DEC 99

Rhymer in the Sunset

Dedicated to the Memory of

My poems are dedicated to the members of
Alpha Company, 1st Battalion (Airborne),
501st Infantry, 101st Airborne Division,
and to the memory of

William N. Lockett	December 30, 1967
Roy L. Winer	February 4, 1968
Danny L. Smothers	March 8, 1968
Bogard L. Floyd	March 16, 1968
Gary P. Hadley	March 16, 1968
Eddie L. Ephriam	March 21, 1968
John R. Horton	March 26, 1968
Roger W. Overstreet	March 27, 1968
Frank L. Rodriguez-	March 29, 1968
Manuel Ruiz	March 29, 1968
Gary A. Scott-	March 29, 1968
Gary L. Young	April 29, 1968
Eddie B. Sands	May 7, 1968
Ellis L. Faircloth	May 8, 1968
Michael J. Fordi	May 8, 1968
John T. Holton, Jr.	July 7, 1968
Wayne E. Timothy	July 23, 1968
Ramiro M. Mora	August 16, 1968

And, lastly, to the memory of Kenny Dyer, who finally lost his battle with Agent Orange. He was the best at walking point. All these, like so many others—wounded, dead and survivors—who suffered so much in the tradition of America, deserve all the tribute we can heap upon them. They may have died in vain, but they lived in honor.

Rhymer in the Sunset

A Combat Soldier's Poetic Perspective of the Vietnam Experience

by

Phillip L. Woodall

Published by
Airborne Press

www.airbornepress.com

Printed in the United States of America
08 07 06 05 04 03 02 01 00 99   5 4 3 2 1

Library of Congress Cataloging-in-Publication Data

Woodall, Phillip, 1949–
Rhymer in the sunset : a poetic perspective of the Vietnam experience / by Phillip Woodall.
p. cm.
Includes index.
ISBN 0-934145-67-9
1. Vietnamese Conflict, 1961–1975 Poetry. I. Title.
PS3573.06125R49 1999
811'.54–dc21   9933968
CIP

Contents

Foreword

In December 1967, 120 paratroopers of Alpha company, 1st Battalion, 501st Parachute Infantry Regiment, 101st Airborne Division, boarded Air Force C141 transports at Fort Campbell, Kentucky, for the long flight to the Republic of Vietnam. I knew it would be bad—just how bad I could not have imagined. For barely a month after we arrived "in-country," as they said back then, we stepped right into the infamous 1968 TET, launched by the North Vietnamese Army and their Viet Cong surrogates, at midnight on the 31st of January. From that night, when our battalion beat back an all-out assault by North Vietnamese regulars, we fought and operated against the enemy for nearly four months—every single day, 24 hours a day, seven days a week—without a single break. It was the worst sustained combat of the war and arguably the worst any unit has gone through in any American war. The casualties were frightful. At the end of those four months, fifteen of us were left out of the 120 who departed Fort Campbell in December 1967. Everyone else had been killed, or wounded so badly that they did not return to combat. And, unbelievably, two of the other rifle companies in our battalion suffered far greater casualties than we did. The pressure was constant and beyond description. It did not take any of us long to realize that the only ticket out of there was made of lead or steel. This was the environment that Phil Woodall and the rest of us found ourselves in.

Alpha Company had more than its share of great soldiers. Our First Sergeant was a combat infantry veteran of Guadalcanal in World War II, the Korean war, and a previous infantry tour in Vietnam. Several senior noncommissioned officers were Korean war vets, and some of our junior noncommissioned officers and soldiers were already going back with us for their second combat tours in Vietnam. Phil Woodall was just a teenager and green as grass but, like so many of those youngsters, he grew up immediately and became as combat-savvy as the most hardened veteran. His courage under fire belied the poet at heart. And, through all the hell, Phil Woodall exhibited a total commitment to his fellow soldiers. His poet's heart demonstrated an unusual humanity and respect toward all human beings—not only his fellow soldiers, but the helpless and tragic Vietnamese civilians caught between us and the North Vietnamese and even the North Vietnamese soldiers themselves, who were doing everything they could to kill us all. Phil was the epitome of all an American soldier should be.

Don Shive

Don Shive is a retired Army LTC after nearly thirty years. A West Point Armor Officer, his military lineage dates back to almost the founding of the country. There is no doubt in the mind of any soldier who has served under him in combat that he could easily have been a general officer had he compromised his integrity. He truly lives by the West Point motto: "I will not lie, steal or cheat nor will I tolerate those who do." He instilled it in his troops and is viewed with a godlike reverence by those who served with him in Vietnam. Most leaders today compromise their way to the top. Not Don.

Preface

This is the place where I'm suppose to explain my poetry. How can I ever do that? I can't: maybe what I can do is share my journey to this point. Writing about 'Nam is like a war in a way. Fortunately for me, it comes in the form of poetry:

Late at night a warrior trembles.
He hears the devil's call.
The clash of Satan's cymbals
Compels a humble awe.
He had killed another man
No thoughts he has can change
His Judeo-Christian demand
That handles victory quite this strange.

Ten months to go and he must be
A warrior extraordinaire
And stand the wrath of an enemy
Lurking in the darkness somewhere.

I write poetry, letters. The pen can be a mighty weapon. Certainly these are powerful forces in the literary wood lines. A doggie (combat soldier) must have a song; the home front and the syndrome have to be dealt with. Watergate and Vietnam weren't honestly explained. Why was the treatment of Watergate more important than the treatment of Vietnam? The impact of 'Nam was by far more real than the exposure of a government scandal. Anybody who says otherwise is naïve. The blood of a warrior was less important to America than the sensation of a scandal. That's part of the home front I can't ignore. One thing a writer must have—and America doesn't have anymore—is perseverance. I believe without Watergate, the perseverance of America might have won out—at least not have lost out. Look at Korea—hell, at least Seoul isn't Ho Chi Minh City.

To me, 'Nam is reality, true reality; the world is a fantasy. Those who complain so vigorously of hard times have a dream world.

A (rice) paddy dream. Nine months on the line (in combat) not to mention nine months in S-3 (operations) taught this old doggie everything you ever wanted to know about the penetration of war.

In the darkness someone lurks
Through a black hamlet maze
A tiger's bite jerks
Closed strong jaws in rage.
Fire! Spring a deadly trap.
Destroy, plunder, pillage
The prey through the map
Has no name for this village.
No name skirmish there minutes long
Brought rage in night magnitude
To seven soldiers brave and strong
With fortunes of vicissitude.
Tiger sprung! Do they dare
Cross a paddy in the rain?
Alert the troops, returning to lair
An ambush has struck again.

I'm still pretty much now the same as then: cynical and sarcastic. After all, I'm a poet. Madness, I say; I am surrounded by insanity all around. Perhaps it is the syndrome that diseases me and drives me into the fermented scavenger hunt for sanity. "Gods of war immortal, slurp the devil's brew. Torch the soul with ferment, bid the pain adieu." All I am is a cursed player who does not know when to surrender, an old soldier preferring death at the Alamo rather than freedom to dress up in a skeleton suit of death and march in protest of some civilized fear.

I am a man now, a parent; accused of passing forth the propaganda of America past that is no longer viable in this educated maze of civilization called everyday life. Don't I know that the only good war story is an antiwar story? Can't I fathom the fact that old "point men" are not glorious but poor victims used by evil men to plunder and murder under false images? Can I not see that my fond memories of war are but nightmares to shun and drive away rightness and goodness of the educated? Can I not see the abounding hard times that injustice and oppression reaps upon the unfortunate?

The world is ready for this warmonger to sheath his sword and denounce what educated America has learned is immoral. I am stained forever as a killer. I must laugh. Not all the one-liners of Bob Hope or the milder swipes of comedians' depictions of Army life are off the mark. I laugh in a different manner: like Carl Sandburg best described, I laugh "as though the Four Horsemen of the Apocalypse were a quartet of fat, merry clowns and war means neither cadavers nor ashes." I laugh because I know the war sting that afflicts soldiers. I know war not from the film of newsmen, but from eighteen months of stealth against a vicious enemy who knows only the barbarism of war and not the neurosis of civilization. I have seen the flashing neons of civilization beckon the unsuspecting to sip from the evils of greed. I have seen the ugliness of prejudice and tasted the burnt emptiness of injustice and inhumanity. But I've also dreamt of diving headfirst into the polluted waters of America just to wash off the crud of war that inundated my body with the unwashable stench of hell. I have forded a canal full of dead fish, seen maggots attack a dead man's brain, felt the pain of leeches sucking at my side.

And I still believe in the America I was born into. I recall early days in Hodgenville, Kentucky, where I grew up in the shadow of Mr. Lincoln, pledging allegiance to the history of fathers who made it possible for this great country to become the super ideological power on earth, a land where people count. Of course I realize it helps being a white Anglo-Saxon Protestant. But hell, I ended up a southerner, which is no claim to perfect heritage. Mr. Lincoln's statue on Lincoln Square in Hodgenville was the portrait of democracy, and Hodgenville was the Bethlehem of America. I was willing to die for his American heritage, but my offering of self to America was scorned by those who were unwilling to hold the imperfections of America sacred at all. I was blinded by propaganda of youth that I could not see—that I was a bad guy led by bad men performing immoral acts. I was too young to hear the sound of hobnail boots on my own feet. Dying at the Alamo was as insane as expecting a civilized America to welcome a warrior home from war with brass bands and ticker tape. The heroes to America were those who split. The college student waving the NVA flag in my face on campus was merely a practitioner of freedom whose right of free speech overrode the barbarian urge I had to kill him. And life goes on. Someday I will learn that I got what I blindly deserved. Countrymen prefer that my sacrifice be viewed as a finality in civilized America, that no other American need be victimized by the evils of war that I suffered. And the only way that can be done is by showing the world that my madness is insane. I am, after all, a poet.

Phil Woodall

Rhymer in the Sunset

Rhymer in the Sunset

Rhymer in the sunset, poet of the seas,
Describing vivid visions of seagulls in the breeze.
Above the crimson Gulf tide, seabirds soar serene;
Red sky joins the ocean, west toward New
  Orleans.
Rhymer is a warrior, one day home from war,
A solitary soldier sitting by the shore;
Reads the words he's written; ebb-tide crashes in;
Stuffs his rhyme into a jar, casts it to the wind.
Then, he sees a mermaid, stroking through the
  brine,
A mirage of beauty swimming, near a danger
  sign.
She swims toward the sunset, a mermaid she
  must be,
Otherwise, a suicide, committed in the sea.

As quickly as she had appeared, she faded out of
  sight,
As if the ocean swallowed her to quench an
  appetite.
The mermaid came to view again with the
  rhymer's Mason jar,
Removed the lid, read the words, gazed inland
  from afar.

"I shed no tears for Jason, my buddy and my
pal.
I see your lifeless body bob in that old canal.
Blood red water, poisoned fish, you took your
final breath.
I prayed to God you would survive the red canal
of death."

"I never gave a eulogy, at least I wrote no verse.
Nothing I could do, my friend, except yell,
scream and curse.
You always called the ocean 'heaven,' Jason, my
good friend.
I'm sending you a letter, perhaps we'll meet
again."

The mermaid sealed the jar again, cast it out to
sea.
She wept while walking in to shore in her brief
bikini.
Few words were spoken between them, little did
they say.
They sat together reverently while daylight went
away.

"Make love to me, dear Rhymer, hold me very
tight,

Speak to me your poetry, help me through the night.
My life had lost its beauty, until I read your rhyme.
Now I see my problem, I'm so selfish all the time."

"O mermaid of the ocean, I've been away so long;
My soul is much too weary to sing a sad love song.
So, what you say, little lady, there's plenty to be seen.
Let's sip old Satan's liquid and prime this war machine."

She laughed, then dried away her tears, stared into his eyes.
They strolled upon the empty beach beneath a starlit sky.
The mermaid and the Rhymer, walking hand in hand,
Listened to the ocean's symphony crash upon the sand.

"Come, my gentle soldier, let's go find a drink.
We'll visit the Gulf Coast Belle, see what you think.

She's a mass of weathered stucco, living past her
prime.
But a hell-of-a-place to tango and have a good
old time."

Beneath a silver ball they danced, upon a hard-
wood floor.
They tangoed and rhumbaed; he put away the
war.
The mermaid and the rhymer boogied to a Latin
sound,
Sharing moments of pleasure with no one else
around.

He wore vestments of glory and paratrooper
boots.
She danced like Carmen Miranda without a hat
of fruits.
They passed a rose mouth-to-mouth, slid across
the floor,
Paused to sip Margaritas, then they danced
some more.

They danced and drank the night away, lost in
each other's eyes.
They walked again upon the beach, warmed by
sunrise.
Two people needed company, sharing what's
inside,
Mermaid and the Rhymer wading in the tide.

BN (AMBL) 501 ABN. INF
BTRY. 1 BN. 321 ARTY.
A BTRY. 2 BN. 11 ARTY.
WELCOME TO
SANDY
M) 501 ABN. INF.
Y 321 ARTY. BN.
Y 2 BN. 11 ARTY.
GERONIMO

A Night of Leeches

"Let's go," screamed Coley.
Why he did would forever haunt him.
The squad leaped from the bird.
His command would long plague him—
Why had they jumped, six of them,
Unto wet and muddy ground,
While trailing birds banked skyward,
And would not set down.
Their bird lost RPM while
Taking heavy fire—
Flew back toward heaven,
Heard an angel choir.
The bird was blown out of the sky
By a foe who raised a cheer,
The stranded squad had no radio,
To ease their isolated fear.

Again instincts had saved Coley,
But no burden had he shed,
He had two men badly wounded,
And two squad members dead.
There would be no rescue tonight
To alleviate the pain.
Murray, Willie, Ralph and Coley
Were drenched by February rain.

Murray died in blackness. Coley knew
right away.
Willie manned his sixty, his thoughts
turned sordid gray.
"O blessed Mary, mother of God,
Don't let this doggie die.
If it ain't so, bless my soul—
Tell mama not to cry.
Ain't been the best guy, I know Lord,
But look where the hell I am—
Stuck in a paddy in the middle of
night,
No longer giving a damn."

The night passed along, chilly, cold,
wet,
From toe to face,
A long weary night of blackness,
Slithering at snail's pace.
Souls of men taught to believe what
America teaches,
Belonged to the devil's forces, this
Rainy night of leeches.

Leeches suck at Murray's wound even
After he's dead:
The squad lay in knee-deep water
keeping
Ralph's head
Above a parasite infested environment
For rice.
Three survivors avoid finality of
Ultimate sacrifice.
Light from morning finally arrived,
Allowing vision,
So birds of Americans in the 101st
Airborne Division,
Can find three warriors in the
Morning mist,
And erase their names from the
Missing-in-action list.

Journal 18 Feb 68

In search of brass bands and ticker tape,
The mighty warriors tread.
A hero's might, a hero's plight,
The musty tombstone read.

A Beacon Will Shine

Lee Ann was lonely, all she could do,
Was offer a thousand tears to shed,
Her sorrows continued to accrue.
Her tears wet the shoulder of a man called Jed.
"The right place, lass with sea-blue eyes,"
Her pain Jed could release.
His beautiful song with no war cries,
Must bring to America peace.

Lee Ann and Jed each saw the light,
Of a land where no soldiers die.
A beacon will shine and surely delight,
As it flashes across the sky,
Guiding them into a land,
Where nobody ever fights,
And justice is the key command,
For every human's rights.

Jed, Jed, Copperhead

Jed, Jed, Copperhead,
Weeps with sadness for the dead.
Peace, peace, no more pain.
Too many soldiers have died in vain.

War, war, end it now,
Jed the Copperhead knows just how.
Mass, mass, heal the sore.
Let the Asians win this war.

Jed, Jed, Copperhead,
Lee Ann, Baby, he will wed.
Peace, peace, victory,
Only for my enemy.

Before the Cannons

Mail call brought word from the world;
"Jodie is moving about."
Only a matter of time before a warrior,
Heard the truth come out.
No cause for alarm, not really.
Though now may be the time,
To send his lady the feelings he has,
Pent up inside his mind.

Dear Lee Ann—
Remember mellow love songs,
Remember Browning's lines,
Days with rippled waters,
And honeysuckle vines.
You and I picked clover,
Standing in the rain,
Before the cannons thundered out
Their hate and grueling pain.

I dream some days of those times,
When you and I were young.
Lost in lives of pleasure,
And songs we heard sung.
Now a flame is burning,
Inside this warrior's head.
Likely will that fire burn on,
'Til I lay cold and dead.

Tomorrow may have rainbows,
Thursday may bring snow,
Whatever skies are doing,
I want you to know—
Hard times may surround me,
But good times are ahead,
'Cause when my woes are many,
I think of you instead.

A Balmy April Four

Lee Ann received a warrior's rhymes,
On a balmy April four.
A spring day down in Memphis,
To be remembered evermore.
It was a day of vengeance,
When a great black king was slain,
By a race-hating assassin,
At a hotel called Lorraine.
Events of the day overshadowed a warrior's
rhyme.
The world was livid at the thought of such a
heinous crime.

Dr. King was now in heaven,
Where guardian angels hum,
The words of freedom chanted,
"We shall overcome."

Lee Ann was surprised that she had cried,
For a man she knew little about,
Except that he called for peace, replied
Fate, only bullets. Black man shout
For justice. Will it soon arrive?
"Hell no, Lee Ann, not until black men
Overcome the shackle and the white man's drive
To weld it closed as a final amen."

With midnight tears still flowing,
She fell in the arms of Jed,
Tonight they'd find peace together,
Jodie took the lady to bed.

The Doubtful Scrawl

Dreams of triumph in a warrior's mind
All that Wingate found,
Unriddle the doubtful scrawl and find,
The body of John Brown.

War and courage, love and death,
Indeed a warrior's maze,
Hated and loved in a single breath,
Until his dying days.

An answer then cannot be found,
Without a heavy cost.
Moonlight plays a gentle sound,
Its lullaby of frost.

Unriddle, unriddle, the Doubtful Scrawl,
Like poor old Wingate tried.
A rhyme would quell the devil's call,
When the sleeping sword had dried.

The Paddy Preacher

God lives in the paddy preacher,
No doubt is there in me,
That the doggie reverend, a rare creature,
Will live forever in eternity.

The cross is never so close to a man,
'Til he humps where legions tread.
A painful stake was nailed to his hand,
Ten years later he arose from the dead.

Now the grunt parson did not really die,
Like a buddy once told a friend,
Shrapnel exploded between his eyes,
And his fate was cast to the wind.

The eighties arrived, the cause is lost,
The blood had dried away.
The paddy preacher had paid the cost,
And still had a little to pay.

A Doggie's Heart

I live in civilization,
Among wealth and lives of ease.
I've spent twelve years of fascination,
Suffering point man's disease.

I still remember very well,
Humping through hard times.
Now the story I must tell,
And write my ghoulish rhymes.

I must sing a warrior's song,
Right off the devil's chart.
Old Satan's beat is mighty strong,
Inside a doggie's heart.

Dream World

A skinny lad from Memphis, Tennessee,
Set out one day to play Old Scratch's game.
He thought he marched to make his country
free,
But found that others could not feel the same.

The cannons roared a symphony of rage,
The armies marched through hardships and in
rain.
Trapped deep inside an Asian's steel-barred cage,
A fury wrapped his lonely heart in pain.

He jetted home and saw a world at play.
He felt an awe he could not understand;
Confused his soul with words he could not say,
He knew deep down a dreamworld lay at hand.

He found a cry of pain and song of fear,
Why was the world not filled with thankful
cheer?

Stone and Steel of Yesterday

Count the graycoat cannons
Dressed in battle line.
Prize an orchard's burgeon
In nineteen eighty-two.

Concede a gunboat's power
Upon a river
Patrolled by bass boats,
With deadly hooks.

Sacred Shiloh!
You bitter blaze of cruelty
Disguised as torch
Of sacrifice.

Can you not hear
The howling pain
Of fuzzy-cheeked youths
Ordered to die?

The Hornet's Nest echoes
A perpetual breath
Of hostile ritual
Raging in the woods.

Stone and steel of yesterday
Is drugged by exhaust
From bizarre machines
Enslaved by modern man.

Poisoned past of minie ball
Reflected on a bloody pond
Cannot be changed by any act
That humans can acclaim.

Who Cares

(A Dorsimbra)

Who cares about Vietnam anymore?
The cause is lost, the blood has dried away.
But those who fought cannot forget their war;
A syndrome stalks them 'til their dying day.
A civilized leopard leaps,
From its concrete perch,
Clawing at a warrior's soul,
With razor-sharp guilt.
Latch the memory shutters of the brain;
Feel the pain, fool, or put the war away.
Nam is buried like steel birds in the sea.
Who cares about Vietnam anymore?

Two Grunts From Salt Lake City

A dozen years have washed away
The Mississippi mud,
Since buddies met the judgment day,
In paddies full of blood.

In sixty-eight when cannons roared,
Two boys became two men,
In Asian heat the devil scored—
"To Hell and Back" again.

Joe and Dan stood side by side,
In paddies and in rain.
With Utah dreams and Eagle pride,
Amidst old Scratch's pain.

Steel birds were buried in the sea,
Indeed a shameful pity.
Buddies came home to the land of the free—
Two grunts from Salt Lake City.

Erase One Day

Few could hear the
song
In the breeze
A bluebird crooned
In an eerie air.

Rifles screamed
A lasting salute
To a buddy laid
In fresh turned grave.

Sadness urged
A warrior's spirit
To surge with
thoughts
Unknown before.

"Farewell, Friend.
Tomorrow I leave
Without you to face
The foe again."

"I shall weep
No more
Lieutenant.
I wept already."

A red clay crown
Of towering pines
Bejeweled a soul
For eternity.

A weeping mother
Leaned upon
Her sullen husband—
Crying.

Booze dulled the pain
Of a warrior's
Black journey
To Georgia.

Family gathered,
And grimly recalled
A fair-haired kindred,
Asleep forever.

Mother hugged
A young soldier,
Acquainted by
Precious letters.

Gentle pleas,
Eased extraction
Of a painful
Song of war.

Destroy Cong
In paddyvilles!!
Beware of
Booby traps.

Sleep in graveyard
Mounds at night.
Hear old Satan
Laugh out loud.

Dragon fire
Lights up the night.
Shrapnel sings
A fatal tune.

A final gasp
Fills the lungs
Of a twenty-year-old
American.

He trained
In Officer's School
To die
Like a soldier.

Sleep in peace
Lieutenant,
Before the cause
Dissolves forever.

The black journey
Faded to battle gray.
A fire of war
Burnt on.

Rocket back to war
Streak across the sky
From civilization
To a lair of hate.

Saddle up, paddy
  warrior.
Forget about worldly
Dreams of rainbows
Glittering at night.

Return to black
  battle.
Leeches are poised
To suck the veins
Of sightless victims.

Blindness attacked
The body with
More blackness
Than eyes had
  known.

Flashing neons
In the night
Were tracers
Spitting death.

Far away,
Rainbows of
  civilization
Twinkled like distant
Stars above the tree-
  line.

Enemy lurked
In the blackness.
Leeches patrolled,
The paddy water.

The only light
In his body
Was unreal,
Far-off dreams.

A tan-skinned beauty
Floated gracefully,
Blonde hair
Hanging down.

Civilization
Was only a dream
Of rainbows
In the night.

Those who sang
Of civilized woe
Were sugar-coated
In a dream.

America was
A munchkin land–
Distant as
A far off star.

Erase one more day
From the cloth
Until the
Count is nil.

Victory
Meant returning
Home to
America.

Dreams evolved
Into the only
Form of civilization
Darkness provided.

One-hour guard,
Two hours sleep,
Darkness dominated
Either state.

Time to move.
March at sunrise.
Saddle up
The devil's mount.

Guerilla!
Stay low,
Get him, get him,
Make him pay.

Shadows return,
When the sun
Fades over
A hundred paddy
warriors.

Lost cause,
Dried blood,
Ho Chi Minh City,
Victim.

Warrior, hear
The bluebird's song
A decade
Still unchanged.

Monks of Phu Vang

There ain't
No slick
Farewell
Lieutenant.

A rippling
Crimson sea
Washes away
Like golden sand.

Stone and steel
Of yesterday
Yearns to whisper
Truth.

We are
The sons of My Lai
Hardly deadly,
Anymore.

Aged, crusty,
Crippled,
Limping,
Toward midnight.

Stalked
By blackness,
Wave so long
Warrior.

Say farewell
To the
Monks
Of Phu Vang

Or,
Bid goodbye
To
Breathing.

How can
I forget
A Buddhist
Bloodbath day?

March
Sixteenth
In nineteen
Sixty-eight,

White robed
Monks lay
Silent
By the trail.

Their deaths—
Too many—
Not the least
Insane.

Who is to blame
For darkness
Or who's
To see?

Point Man

Point man, point man, hump real fast.
Enjoy each breath, it may be the last.
Point man, point man, danger spot.
Crazy when it's peaceful, dead when it's
  not.

Hai Lang, Hai Lang, nightmare town.
Enemy is in there, won't make a sound.
Hai Lang, Hai Lang, lair of hate,
Foe's fortified; he lies in wait.

Gabriel, Gabriel, blow man blow.
Point man cometh, let him know.
Gabriel, Gabriel, horn blares away.
Let him know what stands in his way.

May-Day, May-Day, a natural desire.
He dives for cover. THE FOE OPENS FIRE.
May-Day, May-Day, devil's invitation.
Point man escapes for a brief duration.

Victory, victory, point man performed.
Five enemy captured, he's informed.
Victory, victory, a few got away,
Point man's instincts saved him today.

Point man, point man, goin' insane.
Don't see the glory, do feel the pain.
Point man, point man, what can you do?
Drink lots of whiskey, slurp lots of brew.

A Hundred Paddy Warriors

A hundred paddy warriors,
March toward the sun,
Hunting Victor Charlie,
Camping lots of fun,
Snuggling close to leeches,
Sleeping in the rain,
Laughing in the face of doom,
Going near insane.

Pulling guard at midnight,
And again at three,
Pay no income taxes,
Mailing letters free.
Dreams of perfumed ladies,
Foiled by sniper fire,
A hundred paddy warriors,
High stepping in the mire.

Friendly Fire

Hero,
If so,
I don't know.

Night fight,
Grim plight,
Battle night.

C.O.,
Says go,
Strike the foe.

I say,
Delay,
The foray.

I see,
Friendly,
Cavalry.

My ire,
Inspires,
A cease fire.

Hero,
If so,
I don't know.

The Devil's Seal

He loved poems of battle, rhymes of glory, verse
of war.
He heard distant cannons thunder, saw nervous
horsemen charge;
Now his turn rose for challenge, his time to cross
the bar.
Mighty warrior Coley Hawkins made rhyme
upon a dyke.
A kilometer away, a bomber dove and made its
deadly strike.

Not aghast, this rhymer, he'd seen it all before.
Six months his daily job had been to destroy,
The khaki devil, to flush the varmint out.
Then call the sky invaders and utilize their clout.
He wrote:

"Sky chariots armed with catapults,
Attack the heathen's lair,
Legions now have trapped the prey,
And brought their force to bear."

One bomb hit the paddy, exploding mud into
the sky.
Knee-deep water behind the dike was refuge
from the blast.

Harmless, but quite muddy, the charge one-
  eighth a ton,
Splattered Coley's journal below his words of
  rhyme.
The mud was illustration for a weary warrior's
  verse.

What other words could capture the essence of
  the day?
A mud-splashed poem of four brief lines said all
  he had to say.

"What happened to your poem, man?" Big
  Willie asked and laughed.
He shook his fist defiantly at the jets returning
  home.
He laughed again at the devil's seal—
  the bombers left behind,
A seal of mud upon the rhyme, a legal document;
Ol' Satan stamped the warrior's words,
  "Approved this day in Hell."

Little Dunker Church

Coley found comfort in a blown out Buddha shrine,
A pagoda laced with shrapnel, a temple once divine.
He dreamed about another time, his memory did search,
The photo of Antietam and a little Dunker church.

The Dunkers were a peaceful clan, tillers of the soil.
They watched in horror, terrified, at two armies marching in,
En route to kindle Satan's fire and watch the cauldrons boil;
Boil with death, boil with pain, battle's fearsome plight.
But the generals had it all worked out; there would be a fight.

Confederate dead in the churchyard litter sacred ground.
Union pickets in the cornfield lay lifeless all around.
The photo reveals another sign that Coley understands;
When the armies leave to fight again, the little church still stands.

Rainbows in the Night

(Part 1)

Above the ocean jetting star,
Or man-made satellite?
Inland, neons glitter
Like rainbows in the night.

Flashing signs mimic stars,
Twinkling clear and bright.
Greed, not beauty, is the role,
Of rainbows in the night.

Barefoot imprint upon the sand,
Will soon be washed away.
Monuments of stone and steel,
Stand in the light of day.

The rays of light give focus,
To the human city plight,
And reveal the imperfections,
Of rainbows in the night.

Rainbows in the Night

(Part 2)

Banners darkened, flares extinguished,
Dragons come to sight.
Red and green in darkness flashing
Rainbows in the night.

Tracers spitting, cannons thunder,
Shrapnel whizzes by;
In the dreams of weary warriors,
Dance maidens in the sky.

Sparkling eyes, curls of softness,
Soothe a soldier's sight.
Civilized pleasures unforgotten,
Rainbows in the night.

Need they never, must they always
Wish and hope and pray?
Tender skin, lips of crimson,
Again will pass their way.

Dream on legions, believe the vision,
Forget yesterday's fight.
Have faith in dreams of pretty maidens,
And rainbows in the night.

John Holton

Holton was from Jacksonville,
Amigos, he and I.
Gave me cash to buy some booze,
Waved to me goodbye.

I went to Hawaii
To spend my R & R.
Rest up from the fighting,
And nurse my battle scar.

I walked the beach of paradise,
Civilization I did tap.
Holton humped the boonies,
Tripped a booby trap.

Back came I to battle,
Toting Holton's rum;
I cried when I discovered,
He was blown to Kingdom come.

I sat inside a bunker,
Stared into the dark.
Saw John Holton's image;
A friend had made his mark.

Lee Ann

Lee Ann, baby, far away,
Honey lips, creamy skin,
You are the vision inside my head,
Just want to see you again.

Lee Ann, baby, been so long,
Turquoise eyes, golden hair,
I wish I was home with you in my arms.
Just want to touch you, I swear.

Moonlit night, cool and breezy,
Lovers walking hand-in-hand,
Dreaming of you gives my body strength,
My god, I miss you, Lee Ann.

Captain says, "Saddle up,"
Hurry, hurry, cross the stream.
I hide you away inside my head,
Refueled by my dream.

Lee Ann, baby, ain't goodbye.
C'mon lady, don't you cry.
I'll see you when the birds flock south;
We'll watch the snowbirds fly.

Flesh Wound

There are Cobras in the sunset,
Heading for a fight.
There are "Tigers" in the bushes,
Holding fast for night.

Mortars sing a tune of vengeance,
Whizzing overhead.
AK's chatter in the distance, while
The infantry is fed.
Ham and limas, beans and franks
Pound cake for dessert.
A round explodes, shrapnel flies,
A buddy has been hurt.

The warrior's wound is very slight,
A flesh wound in the back.
"Oh what the hell," the Cap'n says.
"Let's call a Med-Evac."
Lifted out, the soldier grins,
Wishing comrades well.
His bird ascends to heaven;
The grunts remain in hell.

Bleeding hearts, do not weep,
For warriors in the night.
'Tis the enemy who will pay heed,
To the Eagle's dreaded might.

Boonie Rats

Lovely shrine to Buddha,
In a Hamlet south of Hué,
Is refuge from scorching heat,
This stifling midday.

So far, the day's been peaceful,
Despite some sniper rounds,
A paddy march, now some rest,
Inside these hallowed grounds.

Word is out, hot chow en route,
Rest your weary hooves.
Not for long out here, my friend,
Airborne always moves.

Read old mail, change your socks,
Shave, and blow some Z's
A "Homey" from the third platoon,
Comes by and shoots the breeze.

Oh glorious, glorious boonie rats,
Go ahead and dream,
But remember Victor Charlie,
Expect a deadly scheme.

If You Called Her a Lady

The lady strung a trip wire across the village
  path,
Attached it to a hand grenade, proved her
  vicious wrath.
Big Willie saw the lady perform her ghoulish
  work.
He grabbed the VC female, then Jason went
  berserk.

Jason struck the lady, time and time again,
Drew his forty-five, stuck it on her chin;
Pulled the trigger slowly, squeezed a second
  time,
Doc called Jason's actions, "a vicious, heinous
  crime."

Sarge told Doc to "can it," decked Jason with a
  right,
Signaled Willie forward, "deploy his deadly
  might."
The shots from Jason's pistol would surely
  attract,
Curiosity from Ol' Charlie. "Time now to attack."

Doc cursed Sarge's order. "Look what's
happened here!"
Sarge shook his head and muttered, "Let's get
one thing clear.
This lady's friends lurk nearby with terror in their
eyes,
Go on, Doc, move on out, tell 'em we
apologize."

An RPG exploded, capping Sarge's speech.
Doc dove for cover; no longer could he reach
Beyond the pangs of righteousness or the threat
of war;
Doc cried out loud in anguish, "Oh God, how
much more?"

Willie's machine gun chattered a lullaby of
death.
Sarge planned his counterattack without the
least regret.
Jason stared, glassy-eyed, at the lady lying dead.
Doc hid behind a spider hole, "to hell he had
been led."

Sarge directed cannons to pound the deadly foe.
He requested reinforcement on his radio.
"Damn you, Jason," Sarge cursed, "You stupid little jerk,
I'd trapped all them varmints if you hadn't gone berserk."

"Damn it, Sarge," quipped Doctor, "I ain't letting this pass,
Jason is a murderer. I'm going to nail his ass."
Sarge didn't wish to listen, the foe was still at large.
He must deal with Jason, though he preferred to charge.

"I will play your game, Doc, Tell me what is right.
The enemy is out there just itching for a fight.
Jason did go crazy and was stupid, I agree;
But the enemy will go to any length to gain a victory."

"Can't we just quit fighting, Sarge, let the foe alone?
Go back to America, where no more wounded moan."
Sarge did laugh at Doc's reply, "You force me to repeat,
The peace you seek is equally this army's bad defeat."

The army did not punish Jason for killing the VC,
It didn't matter; two days later Jason was set
free.
Not by courts of justice or other authority,
But with ruptured chest from ordnance by the
enemy.

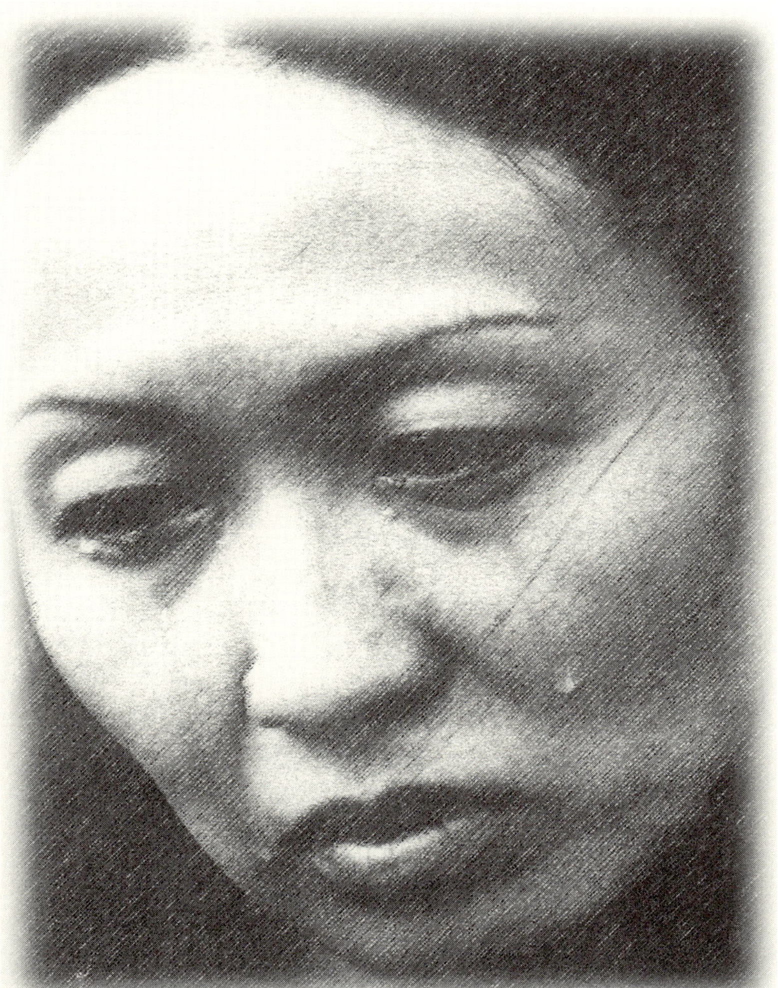

Warrior Cursed a Rhymer

Sunrise o'er the Song Bo,
A calm reflective time,
He scrawls some words upon a pad,
This warrior, cursed to rhyme.

Something deep within him,
Forces rhyme to flow.
This warrior, cursed a rhymer,
Writes his rhyme of woe.

He is neither poet,
Nor literary man,
He's a warrior cursed to rhyme,
Inside a war-torn land.

He is first a soldier,
Then he writes his verse;
But to rhyme about the war zone,
Is indeed a warrior's curse.

Stopover

Bien Hoa, Japan, Alaska,
Long time in the sky,
They wore short-sleeve tropic khakis
With a blizzard to defy.

Twelve long months of battle,
Warm Alaska's chill.
Half hour in the airport lounge,
Gives them all a thrill.

Almost in the world again,
Mere hours to survive,
Freedom bird lands in Oakland,
They all got home alive.

Beneath a Crimson Sea

Shades of blue and grayish clouds
Forewarn lost souls that doomish fate
Would rise above the fluffy shrouds
That shiny treasures could create.

A warrior from decades past
Endured the hardship war uncovered,
Then signed a new-formed plaster cast
Of an injured world he had discovered.

The cause was lost in oceans deep.
Typhoons guarded against return.
Drifting warriors were urged to sweep
Away the cause, watch it burn.

A syndrome became the residue
Of a kindled, flaming, final end,
And all that warriors suffered through
Dissolved in fury, whirled in the wind.

Blow strong wind, gust and gale,
Sting a warrior's face.
The pain of war must soon exhale
Upon a final resting place.

Names etched in stone upon the land,
Signposts for history,
Are washed away like golden sand
Beneath a crimson sea.

Glory Path

Courage be thy watchword,
Brave men must unite.
Cast aside ye scabbards;
Confront the dragon's might.

Slay the fire-breath demon
Whack him with thy blade,
Defy his burning vengeance.
Do not stand afraid.

Legions tall in battle,
Endure the dragon's wrath;
March along old Satan's ledge
Upon a glory path.

Satan's Victory

From the grass between the tombstones,
He watched an eagle soar,
He dreamt of marching armies,
And heard the cannons roar.

The air was filled with shrapnel,
Hungry stomachs growled,
Soldiers fell like bowling pins,
The fallen wounded howled.

In force, the enemy sprung their trap.
Prisoners, they did take.
Drove the hordes unto the pits,
For the devil's sake.

Satan, himself, commanded,
From headquarters in the field.
He nodded his approval,
Of the recent battle's yield.

Matter of Calibration

I hear the cries of youth protesting.
I know the fears, before them they do see.
I feel the pain of a nation divided.
I watch my foe claim his victory.

Now I pine, my head bowed slightly.
I try to suppress a gut-gnawing rage.
I hear the words that hard times confront me.
I shake my head and read the devil's gauge.

My gauge was set in paddy and in jungle.
There, Satan lurked, with power truly great.
How can my gauge record your dissension?
Before it can, I must recalibrate.

The scene is bad, but not a pit of venom.
Hard-core civilization reigns throughout the land.
The devil's here; his forces are not mighty.
The horned imp knows he cannot make a stand.

He's tried before; there was quite a struggle.
The South ran red with blood, guts and gore.
But honor reigned, people reunited,
Upon their land war would rage no more.

A useless loss? Our fathers' blood is vested,
For some ideal few can understand.
Why must we fight in Asia or in Europe?
Can we not cherish peace throughout the land?

In isolation, behind walls of ocean,
Our ideals grow in magnificent conception.
We know we're right; our fathers were in error.
We see clearly, unrighteous imperfection.

We are blinded in our bliss of education.
The peace we seek is easily secured?
Throw away legions past of honor,
Forget the pain our fathers have endured.

We have it worse; we have bombs and missiles.
We can destroy the world our fathers made.
Have we the right to cast aside their honor,
Change the world and watch their glory fade?

The Victim

He endured the bloody battles.
He plunged the deadly sword.
He low-crawled through muck and mire,
And called the devil Lord.
Lord of battle, Satan was,
Anxious to begin;
'Cause when the big guns thunder,
The devil's forces win.

Below, smoke has lifted.
Above, the eagles soar.
He sees the marching armies,
And hears the cannons roar.
A battle brews inside this man,
A warrior from the past,
A victim now, this soldier boy,
The years get by so fast.

No one ever beat him, though,
This former warring grunt.
Until, that is, the Copperheads,
Attacked on the home front.
Righteous zealots, Copperheads,
"Peace," they did repeat.
"Ain't gonna study war no more,"
Is the war cry of defeat.

The warrior fought tooth and nail,
Against the deadly snake.
The Copperheads found victory
In the Watergate mistake.
The NVA were victors,
And, too, the Copperhead.
The hero's cause and glory
Lay buried with the dead.

His pain is deep and chronic,
And will never go away,
Until he finds his glory,
Or Gabriel's trumpets play.
He sought to be a hero,
Like his noble fathers tried,
But he is just a victim now,
Like those in vain, who died.

He will tell his story;
Those who wish to hear,
Will learn of pain and sacrifice,
His fathers held so dear.
Many claim the job he did,
Was useless and in vain;
His journey through the pits
Of hell was totally insane.

It no longer matters to him,
That heroes are not praised,
That crowds no longer cheer
At flags of honor raised.
The victim, indeed, can stand the heat,
The fires inside of hell,
And stand the pain of bleeding wound
To ring old glory's bell.

Ho Chi Minh City

Once he slept in paddies,
Providing leeches blood.
He sought the deadly Viet Cong,
Through heat and fire and mud.
He braved his enemy's terror,
Endured the awesome fight,
Whipped the enemy one-on-one,
With stealth and mind and might.

He would stand not victor,
When the cherished peace arrived.
He's shackled, now a victim,
And of glory is deprived.
Jubilant enemy soldiers,
Victors without pity,
Race war machines into Saigon,
Proclaimed Ho Chi Minh City.

America's young celebrate, too,
Their army's bad defeat.
The warrior's mind is much confused;
He never had been beat.
Jack Daniels to the rescue,
Soothe the pain inside;
Firewater by the gallon
Will drown a warrior's pride.

Farewell glory. Take his sword.
The film proves he's been beat.
A warm spring day in seventy-five,
He finally concedes defeat.
'Tis sad, 'tis sad, this pain he feels,
And stronger it will get,
But a warrior who withstands the pain
Knows he ain't dead yet.

Can You Hear the Clank?

Can you hear the clank of the war
machines,
Speeding down a Saigon street?
Stone and steel sing a sad melody,
A final chorus of defeat.

He heard clanking in his nightmares,
A creaking sound of fear,
Like fingernails scraping a blackboard,
An eerie noise to hear.

Celebrant Asians wave and cheer,
Atop a speeding tank.
He wakes up in a haunting sweat,
Unnerved by the armor's clank.

Freedom Bird Call

Three recoilless rifle rounds
Shot me in the shitter
Sixteen months were long enough
To call this boy a quitter.

Tam Ky, final days
Fifty-nine and counting
Captain Gay blown away
And the fires of a smokeout are mounting.

Look at rainbows late at night
Watch a gunship perform
Seek some shelter for safety
From the wrath of a bloody storm

Facing a full-fledged fury
For nearly five hundred days
Had damaged a kindred spirit
With lightning and thunder displays.

The cupboard was bare, the shingles loose
Time to empty the pockets
Time to believe in a freedom bird call
And look out for enemy rockets.

Ivory Tower

Day after day in the ivory tower,
Gaining some degree of power,
Was not easy to discard,
Or turn his back away.
To heighten his confusion,
Was escape to his illusion;
There were many words of warring,
He knew that he must say.

Character Flaws

Whiskey and women,
Brain is spinnin',
Put my sword at bay.
Write my rhyme,
Drink my wine,
Insanity comes to stay.

Barroom brawls,
Character flaws,
Shape a veteran's story.
Lost in the dark,
Drunk in the park,
Seeking some long lost glory.

Bar Napkin Writer

He sat on his throne,
At Ezekiel's bar,
Sipping a rum and cola.
He chatted with a liberal lady,
About the evils,
Of the Ayatollah.

The point that he made,
In his drunken tirade,
Rhetorical as it might be,
Made left-wingers sore,
With his rumble of war;
Iran was his enemy.

The bar napkin writer,
Did surely excite her.
She ranted and raved at his bunk.
He laughed, then kissed her,
His point had sure missed her,
So all he could do was get drunk.

Excludin' War

Warrior in the ivory tower; seeking glory, man?
Hero on the fortieth floor, God forbid.
No more humpin', eat that gourmet food,
Lovin' it, but gotta tell what that grunt did.

What for, fool, what have you to tell?
Gotta cure a tired spot and march again through
  hell.
Don't know why I "gotta," man, only know I do,
Gotta talk of warring now, just got to.

Don't know why exactly, just believe it, man,
I appreciate capitalism, really like the money;
But ever try to spend cash in the valley or
Buy insurance there? Hilarious, ridiculous, funny.

One thing insurance seldom covers, that, my
  friend, war.
Perhaps that is why my business turns into a
  bore.
I guess the factor of truth I seek turns out to be
Some crazy notion in my head that I'll find glory.

Not too flashy, three-piece vested, Hart,
  Schaffner and Marx,
Four bedroom ranch in the suburbs, couple of
  kids playing ball,
Just don't meet my fancy and I do love kids;
My tired spot aches with pain, that's all.

No common denominator exists for the tower
  and paddies,
Except for the fact I've encountered both.
Comparing shapely working ladies to leeches,
Is likening the beauty of curse words to a
  marriage oath.

I guess I just gotta cuss a little,
Let what's inside me out,
Flash back to my warring years,
And rid my honor of doubt.

Oh Wall

Oh wall oh wall of granite stone
Not tomb or glory chart
Reflects the pain of shattered bone
And shrapnel in the heart.

Mothers moan. Warriors weep.
Abe and George look on
Silent souls would angels keep
Inside the great black stone.

America, America, see
No shining perfect star.
Your undercoat of memory
Reveals an ugly scar.

Remember how the warriors died
In places hardly known.
Remember tears that widows cried
Beside the great black stone.

Ia Drang, Phuoc Yen, Hamburger Hill,
Khe Sanh, hundreds more.
Five thousand days to maim and kill
The victims of the war.

Peace comes now upon the mall
Where painful memories start
To wound those standing by the wall
With shrapnel in the heart.

Acknowledgments

To thank all those involved in the production of this wonderful book of poetry is simply impossible. Although it has been long in coming, it is truly a labor of love. Thanks to Kathryn Autry for her hard work on the Airborne Press Web site. Even when she couldn't understand why something was important to us vets, she persevered. Ruth Lukkari has been a constant inspiration. Her love and commitment and passion for Vietnam vets is unequalled by any other single person I know. Ruth lost her brother in a sister battalion to the author. Her mission is to keep his memory alive. To Diane—her constant support to the poet is nothing short of miraculous. A gigantic thanks to Sue Knopf for her encouragement and inspiration. She has an uncanny ability to take writings written on toilet tissue, napkins, C-rating cartons and turn them into works of art.

Thanks to JA, SJM, the editors at AP, and all those unnamed who have offered encouragement along the way. Thanks to the following for their generous assistance: The Defense Audio Visual Agency, Washington, DC; The Departments of the Army, Navy, Air Force, and Marines. The Vietnam Veterans of America, Washington, DC; *The Army Times,* Washington, DC; and the U. S. Army Military History Department, Washington, DC. The private collections of many of the former soldiers and their families of the 1/501st Infantry Battalion. Specifically Don Shive, former A company Commander in Vietnam; Don Stevenson, now the chief municipal judge in Plano, Texas, and our favorite redleg. First Sergeant Tim O'Connor, now living in Apache Wells, Arizona, probably the best combat soldier any of us has ever known. And a real hero among many, Lee Over. Thanks to the Herculean efforts of John Henkel of Michigan Tech in scrounging up some great photos. Thanks to all the guys of A company, 1/501, 101st Airborne who attended the reunions and to Scotty for putting them together.

We have attempted to use only material for which we have permission, but most vets have collected so many pictures from so many sources, we're never sure. We apologize if we have not credited some person or organization and will make corrections in future printings. Specifically, thanks to those combat soldiers who sent material that we did not use—next time we will: Jim Wodecki, Don Watkins, Dan Pollard, Dennis Mannion, Walter Scott, Casper Johnson, Dan Coy, Jim Kaldor, Ray Stubbe, Paul Knight, Bill Bourgeois, and Bill McBride. Our commitment to the power of the poetry was to assure that illustrations enhanced it and did not detract. We hoped we've accomplished this mission.

Several of the pictures have been generously offered through Vietnam veteran Web sites. The General William C. Lee Museum has also been generous in allowing the use of their archives. A few of the photographs were taken by combat photographers serving in the U.S. military. We thank them for being unsung heroes.

A Selected Bibliography

The mission of Airborne Press is to tell the Vietnam story. Much of our philosophy can be found at our web site, **www.airbornepress.com.** *In light of recent developments in our country, Airborne Press is inextricably opposed to America's continual involvement in the apparent civil conflicts around the globe. We absolutely believe that we should use our resources to assist refugees or displaced persons in whatever way we can and in this we should spare no effort. And the only time military power should be used with deadly force is if someone tries to prevent us from helping. But, we should not be involved in offensive operations in other countries regardless. Our view is HAS VIETNAM TAUGHT US NOTHING? The following selected bibliography reflects our basic philosophy in understanding the lessons of Vietnam. We do not know how many books have been written about Vietnam. In 1993, someone mentioned 500. This number is increasing, and Airborne Press makes an enormous contribution to the literature with Phil Woodall's* **Rhymer In the Sunset.**

NAM. The Vietnam Experience 1965-75. Barnes & Noble, Inc. By arrangement with Orbis Publishing Limited, 1995. (Terrific history of the Vietnam experience. Very good in pictures and conciseness.)

Buckley, William F., Jr.: T*ucker's Last Stand.* Harper Collins, New York, 1990. (Fiction is a great way to learn history and this is a good story of some possible happenings in both Washington and Vietnam.)

Butler, Robert Olen: *A Good Scent from a Strange Mountain.* Penguin Books, New York, 1992. (Something very different and good: Vietnamese voices and their perspectives. One very interesting phenomenon of the Vietnam war is that by and large, the Vietnamese don't hate the Americans, especially the soldiers. This is true also of many vets, who have mellowed even toward their former enemy.)

Carhart, Tom: *The Offering: A Generation Offered Their Lives to American in Vietnam—One Soldier's Story.* William Morrow and Company, Inc., New York, 1987. (A personal memoir, moving and informative. An example of how Vietnam shaped a life.)

Currey, Cecil B., Edward Lansdale, *The Unquiet American,* Houghton Mifflin Co., 1988. (For the serious and thoughtful reader and anyone interested in all aspects of Vietnam, Dr. Currey's books are invaluable. This one gives a picture unseen by other works, especially the early days and what has become known as mission creep. His latest, *Victory At Any Cost, The Genius of Viet Nam's Gen Vo Nguyen Giap,* is a masterpiece of research and insight.)

Dean, Chuck: *Nam Vet, Making Peace With Your Past.* Multnomah Press, Portland, OR, 1988. (A wonderful personal account of one vet's journey. Strong convictions and recommendations toward healing. Excellent reading for families of vets, wives, those in intimate relationships, potential wives or lovers—as fresh for the future as when it was written.)

Emerson, Gloria: *Winners and Losers, Battles, Retreats, Gains, Losses and Ruins From the Vietnam War.* Harcourt Brace Jovanovich, New York, 1972. (A disturbing book in 1972, less so in 1999. A book of perspective, lots of figures, facts: good, a must-read.)

Karnow, Stanley: *Vietnam, A History.* Viking Press, New York, 1983. (History of the Vietnam war, academic and detailed, also a companion for the PBS series, *Vietnam, A Television History,* which will be shown forever.)

Lukkari, Ruth. *And Then There Were Three.* Airborne Press. Publication date, August, 2000. (The first book totally chronicling family grief and the shattering of a family, including its rebirth and passion in keeping alive the memory of a brother who did his duty.)

Lee, John Henry. *Free Fire Zone.* Airborne Press, publication date, November, 2000. (The fictional account of Miles Jacobson, based on actual events. The theme is the transformation of an all-American boy into the epitome of the combat soldier. This is the first of a trilogy.)

MacPherson, Myra: *Long Time Passing: Vietnam and the Haunted Generation.* Doubleday and Co., Inc. New York, 1984. (Possibly the best book written on Vietnam by a non-vet. It just about covers it all.)

Mattison, Lo, Scarseth: *Hmong Lives: From Laos To La Crosse.* The Pump House, La Crosse, WI, 1994. (The Hmong are wonderful people who helped us. We abandoned them, and every American who cares should be ashamed. These are inspiring stories of survivors now in America, attempting to maintain some semblance of their way of life. To the credit of a few Americans, we're trying to help these noble and loyal people.)

Stanton, Shelby L.: *The Rise and Fall of an American Army.* Dell Publishing, New York, 1988. (A wonderful reference with some decided views on how we messed up; mostly the politics of the war. The idea that the entire American Army was sacrificed in Vietnam is not far off the mark.)

Ward, Lukkari, Hamilton, Dobratz: *The Faces Behind The Names.* The Memorial Press, Bloomington, MN, 1996. (A book impossible to read and impossible to put down. One cannot read without becoming emotional at the lost potential. An entire book of short biographies of the fallen written by the families. Although the families are all from one state, Minnesota, the feeling of total representation of all young Americans who never got to live out their lives is very much in evidence.)

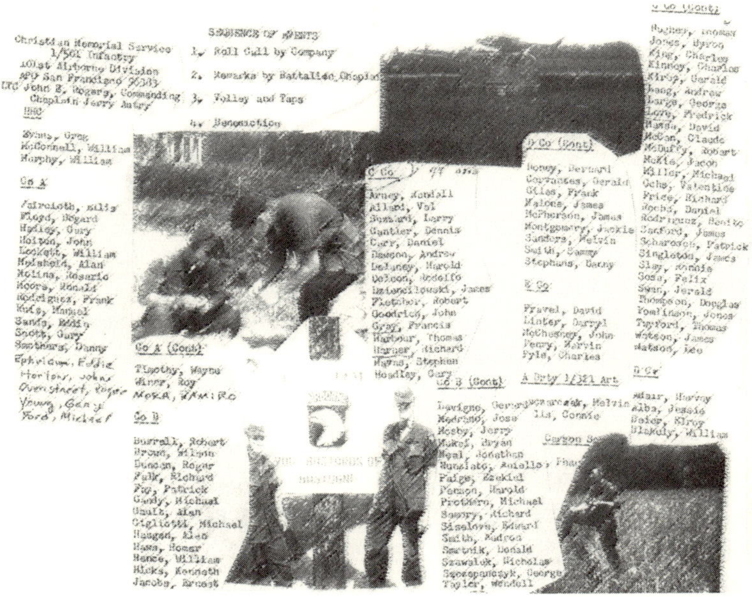

GLOSSARY

This is a general glossary of some words seen in the poetry and others that GIs casually slipped into using. In a war environment, language takes on a property all its own. Here are just a few of those very peculiar words.

ASAP. As soon as possible.

Bird. Helicopter.

Buy the farm. Die.

Booby traps. Insidious devices placed by Viet Cong or NVA in and under almost anything. They could range from very simple devices like grenades to unexploded five-hundred-pound bombs. They became the single biggest fear of the combat soldier, who minded not so much fighting the seen enemy as fighting the unseen one; it became an enormous daily burden.

Cannon fodder. Term used by many GIs to joke about the fact that Eleven Bravos—the infantry; the combat soldiers—were often considered expendable in war.

C's (C-rations). Ready-to-eat meals sealed in metal cans in a carton. Very interesting. Not all that bad and were spoken of more disparagingly than they should have been. Favorites for many were pound cake and peaches, lima beans and ham. Individual likes and dislikes became favorite topics of conversation. Amazingly, GIs could come up with great combinations. C's were heated by C4 tablets, used in explosives.

DEROS. Date estimated to return from overseas. The day the tour was over and return to the world was imminent.

Dorsimbra. A Shakespearean sonnet of four lines, four lines of free verse and a classic sonnet. The first and last lines must be the same. Developed in Memphis during the 1970s.

Dust-off. Medical evacuation helicopter.

Grunt. Combat soldier. A soldier holding the MOS (military occupational specialty) of Eleven Bravo, a combat infantryman.

Grease. Kill.

Hoi Chan or **Chieu Hoi.** An individual communist soldier who turned himself in to South Vietnamese or Americans.

Hooch. Term used to describe Vietnamese peasant huts; sometimes, the Americans referred to their own temporary places as the same.

IP (initial point). Position where a military operation was begun.

Kilo. Radio term used to mean "killed."

Line doggie. Combat soldier serving on the line, the line meaning in a combat zone rather than a support area.

LZ: Landing zone; usually a designated area for helicopters to land.

MOS (military occupational specialty). The soldier's job assigned to him upon entry into the military and very hard to change. In war, most became Eleven B (bravo), combat infantry.

NCO. Noncommissioned officer, beginning with E5, a sergeant.

NVA. North Vietnamese Army.

Paddy. Usually, rice paddy. Soldiers spent a considerable amount of time walking through, standing in and occasionally sleeping in, paddies. Many a night a soldier would wrap his poncho liner about him, lie down to sleep and by morning, the only thing sticking out of the rice paddy would be his nose.

Point man. The first man in a long line of soldiers. Often expected to draw enemy fire.

Poncho liner. The combat soldier's best friend. A lightweight camouflage blanket substituted for all that a soldier missed from home.

PX. Post exchange: a small store, usually set up for soldiers at the base camp.

R&R. Rest and recreation: often time given to soldiers after heavy duty. Most of the time thought of as a specific event, like leaving the battlefield and going to one of several designated spots: Hawaii, Australia, Thailand, or Singapore.

REMF. Rear echelon (use your imagination). A term often given in jest or, on occasion derision, by combat soldiers who were living and dying on "line." Often it took nine support troops to support one combat soldier. The combat soldier didn't resent the support troop and often felt a great sense of pride in his sacrifice. Inequity was a fact of life, however, and this fact can never be forgotten.

RPG. Rocket-propelled grenade; very effectively used by the enemy.

RTO. Radio telephone operator.

Sitrep. Situation report. Often used over the radio.

Sixty. M-60 machine gun.

Slack man. Second man behind point man, who often took up the point man's slack.

Slick. Nickname for the helicopter that combat soldiers most often saw; the workhorse of the Vietnam war.

VC (Viet Cong). The enemy force—mainly South Vietnamese fighting against the Americans.

Webgear. Suspenders soldiers wore to hold equipment, grenades, etc.

Zapped. Killed.

Index of Poems

AIRBORNE
HAVE GUNS
WILL TRAVEL
GERONIMO

Christian Memorial Service
1/501 Infantry
101st Airborne Division
APO San Francisco 96383
LTC John E. Rogers, Commanding
Chaplain Jerry Autry

SEQUENCE OF EVENTS

1. Roll Call by Company
2. Remarks by Battalion Chaplain
3. Volley and Taps
4. Benediction

HHC

Evans, Greg
McConnell, William
Murphy, William

Co A

Faircloth, Ellis
Floyd, Bogard
Hadley, Gary
Holton, John
Lockett, William
Meisheid, Alan
Molina, Rosario
Moore, Ronald
Rodriguez, Frank
Ruiz, Manuel
Sands, Eddie
Scott, Gary
Smothers, Danny
Ephriam, Eddie
Horton, John
Overstreet, Roger
Young, Gary
Ford, Michael

Co A (Cont)

Timothy, Wayne
Winer, Roy
MORA, RAMIRO

Co B

Burrell, Robert
Brown, Wilson
Duncan, Roger
Falk, Richard
Fay, Patrick
Gandy, Michael
Gault, Alan
Gigliotti, Michael
Haugen, Alan
Haws, Homer
Hence, William
Hicks, Kenneth
Jacobs, Ernest

Co B (Cont)

Lavigne, Gerard
Medrano, Jose
Mosby, Jerry
Mukai, Bryan
Neal, Jonathan
Nunziato, Aniello
Paige, Ezekiel
Penson, Harold
Prothero, Michael
Samory, Richard
Sizelove, Edward
Smith, Audron
Smrtnik, Donald
Szawaluk, Nicholas
Szczepanczyk, George
Taylor, Wendell

C Co 44 DEAD

Arney, Randall
Allard, Val
Buzzard, Larry
Cantler, Dennis
Carr, Daniel
Dawson, Andrew
Delaney, Harold
Deleon, Rodolfo
Dziencilowski, James
Fletcher, Robert
Goodrich, John
Gray, Francis
Harbour, Thomas
Harner, Richard
Havas, Stephen
Hoadley, Gary

C Co (Cont)

Hughes, Thomas
Jones, Byron
King, Charles
Kinney, Charles
Kirby, Gerald
Lang, Andrew
Large, George
Love, Fredrick
Massa, David
McCan, Claude
McDuffy, Robert
McKie, Jacob
Miller, Michael
Ochs, Valentine
Price, Richard
Rocha, Daniel
Rodriguez, Benito
Sanford, James
Scharosch, Patrick
Singleton, James
Slay, Ronnie
Sosa, Felix
Swan, Jerald
Thompson, Douglas
Tomlinson, Jones
Twyford, Thomas
Watson, James
Watson, Lee

D Co

Adair, Harvey
Alba, Jessie
Beier, Elroy
Blakely, William

D Co (Cont)

Boney, Bernard
Cervantes, Gerald
Giles, Frank
Malone, James
McPherson, James
Montgomery, Jackie
Sanders, Melvin
Smith, Sammy
Stephans, Danny

E Co

Fravel, David
Linter, Darryl
McChesney, John
Penry, Marvin
Pyle, Charles

A Brty 1/321 Art

Owczarczak, Melvin
Wells, Connie

Kit Carson Scout

Sanh, Phan

Colophon

This book was created using Quark 4.04 for page layout and PhotoShop 4.0 for scan adjusting on a Power Mac G3 by Sue Knopf, Graffolio, La Crosse, Wisconsin.

Fonts are from the Adobe Syntax family.

Paper is acid-free 55-pound Writers Offset natural.

Printed and bound by McNaughton & Gunn, Saline, Michigan.